This book
is in the care of:

India, Lydia, Shawn, Elijah
Woodward

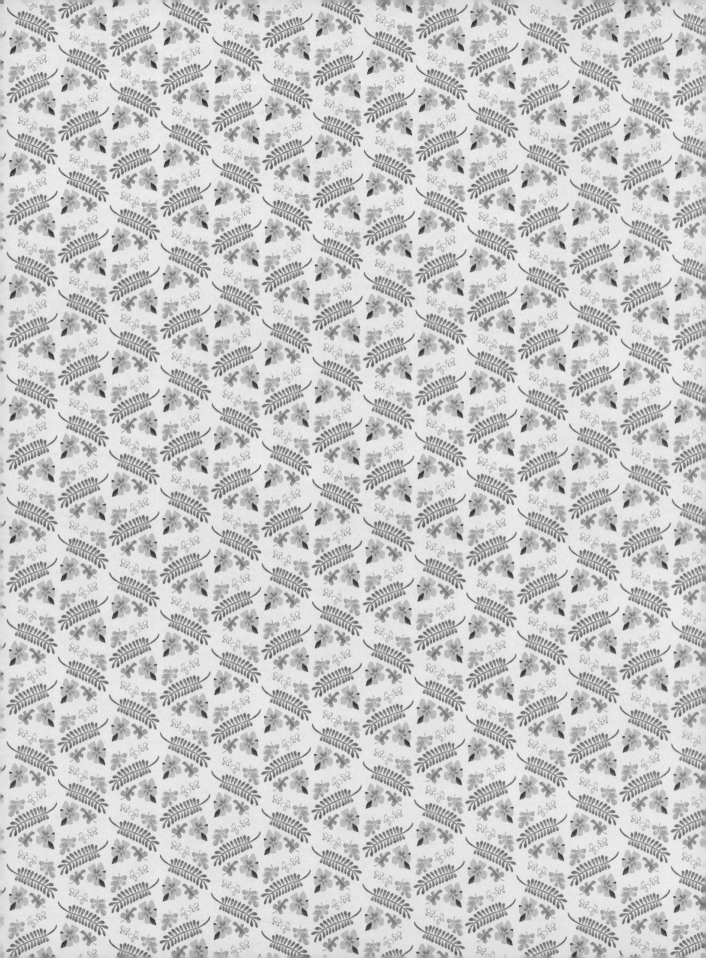

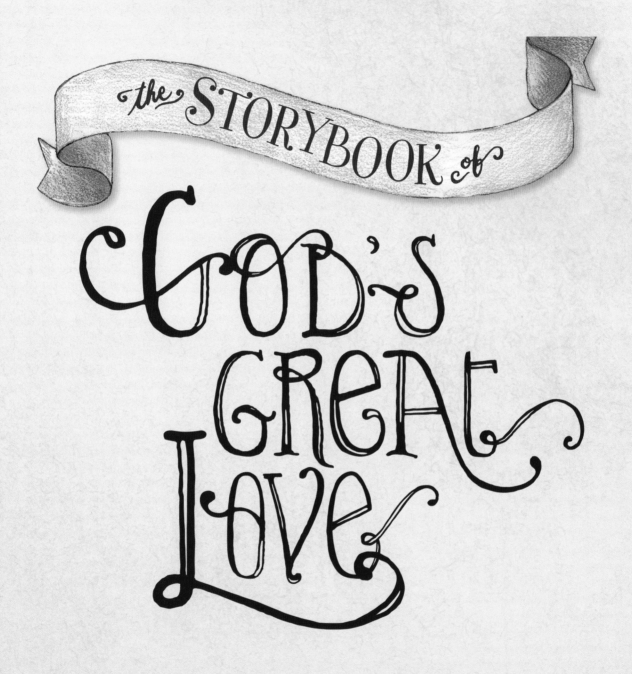

The STORYBOOK of GOD'S GREAT Love

Written by LAURIN GRECO ✳ *Illustrated by* JEFF GREGORY

FOREWORD BY CHARLES F. STANLEY

The Storybook of God's Great Love, Volume II: The New Testament
Copyright © 2016 In Touch Ministries
Text Copyright © 2016 by Laurin Greco
Illustration Copyright © 2016 by Jeff Gregory
Edited by James Cain

 InTouch Ministries
P.O. Box 7900
Atlanta, GA 30357
intouch.org

TABLE of CONTENTS

FOREWORD

"When the fullness of time came" (Galatians 4:4). That's how the apostle Paul described Jesus' entrance into our world. In other words, God had been arranging history for His Son's coming, making sure that everything was just as it needed to be in order for His plan of salvation to come to fruition. The family line of King David had wound its way down through the centuries and come to a point with a young virgin and her fiancé, Joseph. Before Jesus was to be born, a worldwide census brought the couple to Bethlehem (Luke 2:1). Even the stars, in their paths across the sky, announced the Lord's coming (Matthew 2:2).

But to any casual observer, the timing must have seemed off. There was no palace prepared for the King of the universe. The only courtiers to receive Him were shepherds, and the only cradle available was a feeding trough. But Jesus came all the same, and through His life, death, and resurrection, revealed God's goodness and love to the world.

This book recounts the ministries of Jesus and the early church. My prayer is that you will set aside time to read these stories with your children or grandchildren. And when you've read through them once, I hope you'll go back and do it again. Nothing is more important than introducing the next generation to Jesus Christ. No matter how busy your days, no matter how difficult your circumstances, trust that God, in "the fullness of time," has brought you and your child to these moments together to draw you closer to Him.

Charles F. Stanley

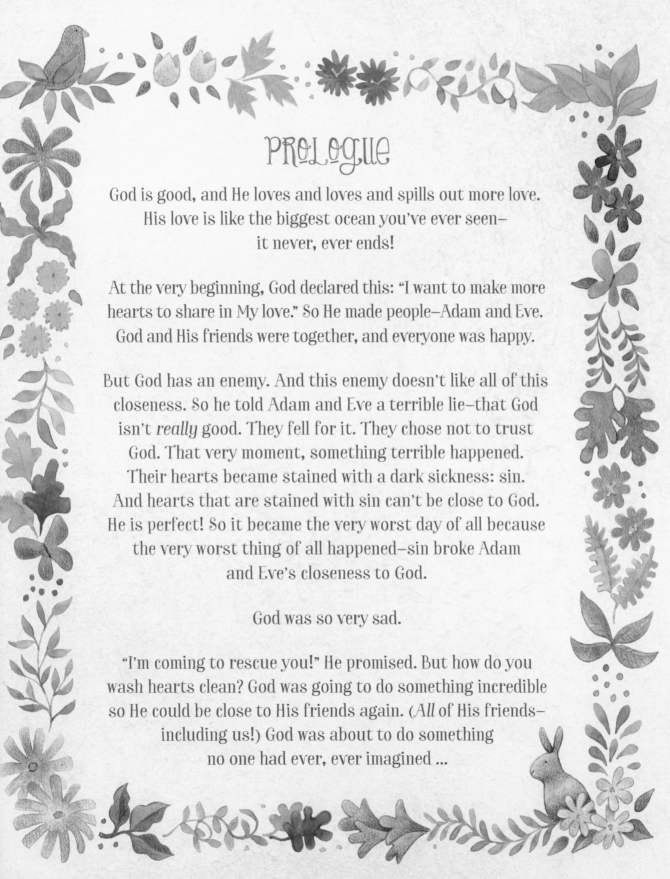

PROLOGUE

God is good, and He loves and loves and spills out more love.
His love is like the biggest ocean you've ever seen–
it never, ever ends!

At the very beginning, God declared this: "I want to make more
hearts to share in My love." So He made people–Adam and Eve.
God and His friends were together, and everyone was happy.

But God has an enemy. And this enemy doesn't like all of this
closeness. So he told Adam and Eve a terrible lie–that God
isn't *really* good. They fell for it. They chose not to trust
God. That very moment, something terrible happened.
Their hearts became stained with a dark sickness: sin.
And hearts that are stained with sin can't be close to God.
He is perfect! So it became the very worst day of all because
the very worst thing of all happened–sin broke Adam
and Eve's closeness to God.

God was so very sad.

"I'm coming to rescue you!" He promised. But how do you
wash hearts clean? God was going to do something incredible
so He could be close to His friends again. (*All* of His friends–
including us!) God was about to do something
no one had ever, ever imagined ...

CHAPTER ONE

GOD'S FAMILY TREE

God had a plan to save you, right from the start.
Matthew 1, Luke 1:26-38

After Adam and Eve sinned—and the whole world broke—God made an important promise.

"One day," He told that sneaky serpent, "a King will show up to fight you. You will hurt Him, but He will squash you, once and for all, and rescue My people."

God promised to fix the broken world and put an end to the serpent's tricks! But God didn't start this great mission by putting on a superhero's cape. Instead, He planted a tree—a family tree—that grew and grew over thousands of years. And as people in His special family lived and died over years and years, God was working on His rescue plan.

It began when Adam and Eve had children. The family tree grew as those children had children, and so on until Noah was born. And God rescued Noah and his family in the ark. One day, God would make a way for everyone to be rescued.

The tree grew, and more children were born, until Jacob came along, and God helped Jacob make peace with his brother. One day, God would make peace with the world.

And Jacob had Judah, whose many-greats-grandson was King David, who saved Israel and was a mighty and good king. One day, God would show the world that He is the mightiest and best King.

God never forgot His promise to rescue His people. As years passed, God kept growing His family tree. He was making sure that one special branch—Noah's branch and Jacob's branch and King David's branch—was growing toward something. Well, toward Someone. And God's plan for that Someone started to take shape when a man named Joseph fell in love with a girl named Mary.

One day, after Joseph and Mary had decided they would get married, Mary received the biggest of *wow* surprises.

"Hello, Mary!" boomed a powerful voice. "God is with you, and He loves you very much."

An angel was visiting, one of God's messengers! Mary's heart pounded. *Thumpety-thump-thump.* Her knees shook.

"Don't be afraid, Mary," the angel continued. "I am Gabriel, God's messenger, and I have wonderful news! God has a plan to rescue the world. He is going to give you a baby—a baby boy. Call Him Jesus, because this baby is God's very own Son, the fruit of God's family tree! He will be a powerful King, like King David, and He will rule his kingdom forever and ever!"

Mary grinned, then gulped, then scratched her head.

"How can I have a baby when I'm not married yet?" she asked.

"Don't worry!" the angel answered. "God can do anything! He will take care of you."

And Mary believed the angel, and trusted. "I want to do whatever God says," she told the angel. "Let Him write the story of my life exactly the way He wants to."

God hadn't forgotten about Joseph! Brave Joseph saw an angel in his dreams, who told Joseph all about God's plan and baby Jesus. Together, Joseph and Mary would play their part in God's great story—as mommy and daddy to a cooing, drooling, bouncing baby boy!

And the best part of the story is Jesus' name, because it shows that God remembered His promise from all those many years ago. Jesus means *"God rescues."*

God rescues. Of course. Because He does.

CHAPTER TWO

THE HAPPIEST BIRTHDAY OF ALL

When Jesus came to earth, it was an invasion of His kingdom.
Luke 2:1-21

"Chirp, chirp, chirp," sang the crickets—a lullaby for the sleepy sheep. Near the town of Bethlehem stood some shepherds, doing the same job they did every night—watching over their fluffy flocks, their eyes wide in the darkness.

Suddenly, the brightest of bright lights appeared—an angel, shining with God's glory! And as it drove away the darkness, the shepherds were scared, scared, *scared*.

"Don't be afraid of me!" the angel said. "God has sent me to bring you the greatest news, news that will make people all over the world so happy! Today, the Rescuer—the One who is going to save you—has been born right here in David's town. It's the happiest birthday of all! It's true! You'll know it's true because you will find this baby wrapped up

safe and lying in a manger, where animals get their food."

All of a sudden, even *more* angels burst onto the scene. It was an angel party! Their joyful song filled the sky, and they sang to God in a voice more beautiful than any you've ever heard. "God is so wonderful! God is so good! And may His peace be with all people because He loves them so much!"

And then the angels went back to heaven. The night was quiet again, and even the crickets were silent with wonder! The surprised shepherds stared at each other, until—"Let's go into town!" they said. "We must see what God has told us about!" And off they ran.

Joseph and Mary were in Bethlehem, too. The proud emperor of Rome was counting everyone, and the village was packed with people who had come home to be counted. All of the houses were full, so Joseph and Mary stayed in a stable, where the animals slept on winter nights.

God guided the shepherds right to where Joseph and Mary were staying. They peered inside, and sure enough—Mary held the baby, God's very own Son! You'd think the Son of God would sleep in the most comfy baby bed, wrapped in the softest blankets in all the world. Instead, Mary laid the Rescuer of all in the animals' food box, just like the angel said.

"You won't believe what we saw!" The shepherds could hardly talk fast enough. They told Joseph and Mary all about the angel party. Mary tucked the story away in her heart, so she would always remember.

The shepherds visited for a while, and then they made their way

back to their flocks, leaping and laughing for joy. They told their story to everyone they met. "God has sent His Rescuer to save us!" they said. "He is here! He is finally here!" And everyone who heard praised God because He was keeping His promise.

When the angels appeared to the shepherds, their bright glory-light scattered the darkness around them. The whole world was dark and broken because of sin, but Jesus left His king-throne to chase away the darkness. His light showed us how much we need God, how much God loves us, and how to follow God's ways. Jesus showed us what His good kingdom will be like, full of joyful light, where there's no sadness and no ouch.

But He started out as a baby, a teeny, tiny light in a dark stable, on the happiest birthday of all.

CHAPTER THREE

GOD'S UP AND DOWN DAYS

Jesus always does just what God says.

Matthew 3-4; Luke 3-4

Splish, splish, splish. John waded in the Jordan River. John was Jesus' cousin, and God had given John a very important job: to get the people's hearts ready for Jesus.

So every day, John stood before all sorts of people and told them to follow God's ways. "Be kind to others!" John called out today. "Because God is kind. And God tells the truth, so don't tell lies–be honest! Let's be like Him."

As John spoke, people remembered how they disobeyed God. Their hearts were broken because they were breaking God's heart. They asked John, "What should we do? How should we follow God?"

"If you want to change and live the way God wants you to live," he answered, "come! Come into the river with me." John lifted some river water in his hands. "When you go down into the water, remember that only God can wash your heart clean. And when you come back up, remember that God gives you new life–a life you can live with Him!"

The people wondered if John was the Rescuer that God had promised. "I'm not," he said. "But I'm clearing a path for Him, and He will be here soon. I just wash you with water, but He will truly wash your hearts!"

Day after day, John would go down to the Jordan River and tell people to turn back to God. So many people did! "Down in the water to wash clean! Up to live a new life!" John would say as he dipped each person in the river. John was baptizing people. He was baptizing so many people that they gave him a funny nickname—John the Baptizer!

One day, Jesus came to the river. He wanted John to baptize Him, too. "No, no, Jesus!" John protested. "You need to baptize me!" Jesus always did what God wanted Him to do. He never sinned, so He didn't need to be washed clean. He was the one who was going to wash people clean—forever.

"God wants everybody to be baptized—and I will do everything God wants," Jesus answered.

"That's how My work will begin."

So *splish, splish, splish*, the two men walked into the river. "Down into the water," John said, just as he had done so many times before. But when Jesus came up from the water, something happened that had never, ever happened before. The sky opened wide, like a curtain over the windows of heaven! A beautiful white dove came fluttering down, until it landed right on Jesus. And everyone heard a voice say: "This is My very own Son. I love You, Son. And I am very proud of You." God was speaking, and the dove showed that God had sent the Holy Spirit, too! The kingdom of heaven was coming to earth!

A little while later, Jesus went into the desert to pray. While He was there, He didn't eat a single thing. And when 40 days had passed, an old enemy showed up to try to cause trouble.

That enemy's name is Satan, and this time, he didn't disguise himself as a serpent. But he still tried to get Jesus to believe the same old lie he told Adam and Eve—"Trust me, God isn't good." But Jesus did what Adam and Eve didn't do. When sneaky Satan told Him lies, Jesus remembered the truth.

"Aren't you hungry?" Satan suggested first. "Make bread from these stones! Do what *You* want."

"No," Jesus said. "God will take care of Me."

Satan tried again. "God loves You, right? Let's see how much!"

"No," Jesus said. "I won't test God's love."

And Satan tried *again*. "Follow me! I can give you better things than God can, even the whole world!"

"No," Jesus said. "I will follow God and only Him."

After that, Satan knew he had lost, so he ran away from Jesus. Satan had tried to be king, but the real King had come! Jesus had come to rescue the world, and He would listen only to His Father's voice and do everything that His Father commanded.

Satan has been God's enemy for a long, long time. He doesn't want anyone to believe God. Or trust Him. Or love Him. And He doesn't want *anyone* to know that God loves them. He'll do anything he can to keep us from God, so he lies all the time.

But God is way more powerful than Satan. And remember God's promise? Jesus came to earth to squash the serpent and show just how powerful God's love really is. And He started His work by obeying God.

CHAPTER FOUR

JESUS' BIG NEWS

Jesus came to make the world look more like heaven.
Luke 4

When *Jesus left the desert,* He went back to His hometown. On the Sabbath (we call it Saturday), He went to the synagogue just like He did every week.

Synagogue was a lot like church. People worshipped God together, praying, singing, and reading His Word. Each week the people would read a part of the Bible out loud—the same part they'd read that time last year. On this day, Jesus was asked to be the reader.

A worker at the synagogue handed Him a long, rolly scroll, and Jesus took it and stood up. The scroll was filled with words that God had given a prophet named Isaiah who lived long ago. (Prophets tell the people what God says.)

After Jesus unrolled the scroll and found the place to read, He read these words: "God's Holy Spirit is living inside of Me, and He has given Me a mission: to bring good news to people who have broken hearts. I will be a Rescuer for people who are stuck because of their sin. Blind people will see, sick people will be healed, and others will go free. So that everyone will know that God loves them."

When Jesus finished, He rolled up the scroll, returned it to the synagogue

worker, and sat down. Every person in the synagogue was watching Him. Then Jesus said, "What I just read has come true—right here, today."

Those people who were listening looked around. They lived in a broken world, just like we do. They saw sickness, sadness, and sin everywhere. In God's kingdom, no one is sick, no one is sad, and sin

is nowhere to be found. Jesus brought good news: He was the King, and God had given Him a mission to bring God's kingdom to earth. God's kingdom was on the way!

So Jesus started to show people how the world could look more like His kingdom! He left the synagogue and went with His friend Peter to another town. There they found Peter's mother-in-law (that's his wife's mom) sick with a high fever. She lay in bed, feeling terrible. Jesus' friends asked Him to help.

Sickness isn't a part of God's kingdom. It's here because this world is broken. But Jesus showed everyone that God's kingdom was coming.

Jesus stood next to her and said in a firm voice: "Fever, get out! You don't belong here!" And right then, the fever went away! She was healed!

Peter's mother-in-law didn't wait. With the fever gone, she looked around and said, "Oh, you must be hungry!" She got up and started to prepare them some food. (Isn't that just what a mom would do?)

And the healing didn't stop there. People from all over town heard that Jesus was healing sick people. While the sun was going down, crowds of sick people came to Peter's house to see Jesus. People with hurting bodies. People with hurting hearts. What a sad parade!

Sick people came for hours. But what started as a sad parade ended happily, because Jesus helped everyone! Person after person came to Jesus sick and hurting, and person after person went home well and happy. They came crying, and they went home laughing. That is what God's kingdom looks like. Jesus, heaven's King, had come!

CHAPTER FIVE

WHEN JESUS GOES FISHING

God wants you to be His close friend and follow Him.
Luke 5:1-11

The Sea of Galilee lapped against the shore, but no one seemed to care. Jesus was there! Any time people were near Jesus, their hearts did something wonderful–they filled with warm love. He stood on the shore that morning, teaching the people about God and His kingdom, and crowds of people all gathered around Him.

Some fishermen sat nearby, too, washing their nets as they listened. They had fished all night but hadn't caught one single thing. Not even one floppy fish!

Jesus stepped into one of the boats on the shore. It belonged to His friend Peter. And Peter was so excited because Jesus was in his boat! Peter dropped his net, sprinted to the boat, and climbed in with Jesus.

"Friend," Jesus said, "can you push away from shore a bit?"

"Of course!" Peter answered, and got to rowing right away.

Splish, splish, splish. When they were a little

way from the seashore, Jesus began to talk about God and His kingdom. The lake was like a big microphone–everyone could hear Jesus even more clearly than before.

After Jesus finished teaching, He turned to Peter and said, "Friend, go out to where the water's deep. Throw your nets into the water, and I'm sure you'll catch some fish."

"Sir," Peter answered, "we were out fishing all night long. And we didn't even catch a single fish! But because it's You asking, we'll give it one more try."

Peter called his fishing team over and off they rowed. When they reached deep waters, they heaved their nets over the side of the boat and into the water. *Splash!* Right away, something odd happened–the ropes grew tight as the nets grew heavy.

Fish! There were fish in the net! And as he helped to pull the ropes,

Peter could tell there were lots of fish in the net! "Ha! Get 'em boys!" Peter shouted. Then he realized he had a problem. There were so many fish that they were ripping his nets!

"Help!" he shouted to the shore. "John! James! There are too many fish for us! Come and help!"

The other fishermen jumped into their boats and rowed as fast as they could. Together the two boats hauled in the nets, dumping pile after pile of flopping fish into their boats. It seemed every fish in the lake had gotten a message to come to Peter's nets. And maybe, just maybe, they had!

Soon they had so many fish that the boats started sinking! The men rowed back to shore, their boats full with fish, and their hearts full of wonder. Who was this Jesus who could even tell fish what to do?

When Peter arrived at the shore, he fell down in front of Jesus.

"Jesus, You're not just good–You're too good!" he exclaimed. "I'm not good enough to be near You!"

Jesus smiled. You see, Jesus knew everything about Peter, just as He knows everything about us. He knew that Peter's heart was stained by

sin. But Jesus loved Peter anyway, and He came to wash hearts clean.

"Don't be scared, Peter," Jesus replied. "I want you to be My close friend. Follow Me, and instead of catching fish, you'll learn to catch people!"

When you get an invitation like that from Jesus, you take it. So Peter, his brother Andrew, and his friends James and John left everything behind. Their boats, their nets, and the huge piles of flippy, floppy fish. Eight other men followed Jesus, too—Philip, Bartholomew, Thomas, Matthew, another James, Jude, Simon, and Judas. We call these friends the Twelve Disciples.

Just like Peter and John and the rest of Jesus' friends, you can take Jesus' invitation. He invites you to follow Him and be His friend. You can spend time with Him, talk with Him, share everything with Him, just like you would your very best friend. And because He loves you so very much, He wants to be your closest friend not for a little while, but forever!

CHAPTER SIX

THE DAY JESUS WASHED A HEART

Jesus wants to make your heart like new.

Mark 2:1-12

"*Today's a big day!*" a man said to his friend, who lay on a mat. "Jesus is in town and we know—we just know!—that He will fix your legs."

You see, the man on the mat couldn't walk. Not a single step. His legs didn't work. So four of his good friends carried him on his mat anywhere he wanted to go.

And today, he wanted to see Jesus.

"Ready, everyone?" another friend called, taking his corner of the man's mat.

"Ready!" the others answered, each grabbing his own corner. And off

they went to see Jesus!

Jesus was teaching at a house, and it was easy to figure out which one. People surrounded it! Inside, the room was packed with so many people that hardly anyone could move without elbowing another person in the ribs! Right in the middle of it all sat Jesus, teaching about God and His good heart.

As soon as they saw the house and the crowd, the friends knew they had a big problem. There were too many people for them to reach Jesus!

But they didn't give up. "We can't go through, so we'll have to go over the crowd!" one friend whispered, pointing to a narrow staircase that led to the house's roof. Carefully, carefully, the four men carried their friend up, up, up to the roof.

"Okay, friends, we'll have to dig to reach Jesus! Let's go!" And together, the friends started peeling back the sticks and clay tiles of the roof.

Inside, Jesus kept teaching. But then a little sunbeam shined down right in front of Him. And then a little dirt tumbled down the beam.

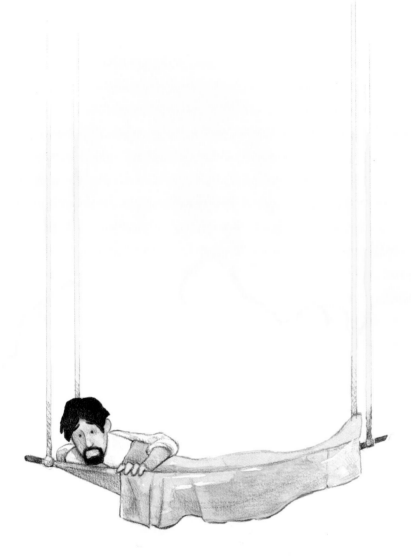

And then more light. And more dirt. The sunbeam in front of Him grew bigger and bigger until Jesus stopped talking and looked up, smiling. Four faces peered down at Him through a hole in the roof!

"Steady, boys!" He heard someone say, and then something big blocked His view of the sky. Down it came, lower and lower. He saw it was a mat. And then he saw a man on the mat! His friends lowered him until he came to rest in front of Jesus. He could see that Jesus' eyes were bright, and his smile was bigger than ever.

"Friend," Jesus said, "I forgive you for all of your sins."

The people whispered to each other, and the religious leaders were grumbling in their hearts. *Only God can forgive sins,* they were thinking. *And this man is not God!*

But Jesus knew all of their thoughts—just like He knows all of ours. "Why are you thinking mean things?" Jesus asked them. "I am God, so I can forgive sins. But since you can't see sins being forgiven—that happens on the inside—let me show you something you can see. Maybe then you'll believe that I am God."

Jesus turned to the man on the mat. "Friend," He said, "get up and walk!"

The man wiggled his toes. They moved! Then he stood up. His legs held steady! Then he started to walk. His legs worked! He skipped, he jumped, he danced—and a cheer came from his friends watching through the hole in the ceiling. He was healed!

Everyone at the house was amazed as the man picked up his mat, joined his friends, and walked himself right back home. "Wow! We've never seen anything quite like this!" they said.

It's true, the man's legs didn't work. But Jesus saw the man's biggest problem: His heart was sick with sin. The man needed his legs to be healed, but he needed a healed heart even more.

Just like the man in this story, you were born with a sin-sick heart. You need your heart healed and washed clean, too. But guess what? You can't do that yourself. Jesus is the only One who can do it. He wants to heal your heart and forgive all your sins, so you can be His friend forever! That's why He came to this broken world—to fix broken legs (and other things!) and to heal sin-sick hearts. Thank You, Jesus!

CHAPTER SEVEN

WHEN JESUS PUT THE STORM IN TIME-OUT

You can trust God, even when you're scared.

Mark 4:35-41

*J*esus stood on the shore of a big lake, and another huge crowd had gathered to hear Him teach about God and His kingdom. After a few hours, it was time for everyone to go home and go to bed. The disciples and the people said their goodbyes.

"Let's get in the boat and head to the other side of the lake," Jesus said. And off they went!

What a nice night to be on the lake! *Splash, splish, splash* went the

bars. Jesus was so tired from His day, so He got comfy on a cushion and soon fell fast asleep.

But the lake didn't stay nice for long. Suddenly, the wind picked up and filled the sails. Then the wind picked up some more. The sails stretched out a little further, and the little boat began to rock in the waves. The wind picked up even more, and the sails seemed ready to pop. Waves as big as a car tossed the boat up and down, to and fro. It was like riding an angry camel!

"There's water in the boat!" one of the disciples yelled as another wave crashed over the side of the boat. "We're going to sink!" another called out. The waves pounded and seawater went everywhere. The men

were sopping wet, and they could hardly see! Sloosh, whoosh!

Everyone on the boat was in a panic. Well, everyone except Jesus. Jesus was still fast asleep on that comfy cushion.

"Jesus, Jesus! Wake up!" a disciple hollered, shaking Jesus on the shoulder. "Help! We're going to drown! Don't You care about us?"

Calmly, Jesus stood up. He looked out at the wind and waves and spoke right to the storm. "Stop!" And the storm listened. The sails collapsed as the wind died down. The waves calmed down, too, until the seawater

seemed like a pane of glass. It was as if Jesus had told the storm to go to time out.

Drip, drip, drip was the only sound you could hear. The water dripped from the disciples' clothes, and their beards. Jesus' friends looked at the sea. Then at each other. Then back to the sea again.

"Why are you so scared?" Jesus asked His friends. "Did you forget that I am good and I love you? Did you let your fears get bigger than Me?"

The disciples' jaws dropped. *The wind and the waves and the sea and the storms know Jesus' voice,* they thought. *Even they obey Him. He must be really, really important.*

Storms can be big and scary. Sometimes storms are made not of wind and waves, but of hurtful and hard things. But Jesus is stronger than them all, and He loves you very much.

So when you're scared, remember how good and loving Jesus is. Remember the wind and the waves know His voice and listen to Him. Sickness and suffering do, too. Nothing–absolutely nothing–is stronger than He is.

And remember how much He loves you. When God thinks of you, He gets a great, big smile on His face! God loves you so much, and He is always going to take care of you.

When a storm comes your way, ask Jesus to make it quiet–because He can. But even if He doesn't, know that He is still up to something good because good is all He can be. The wind and waves of the storm might still swirl all around, but Jesus will hold you in a great, big hug. He will give you peace. And when you're in Jesus' arms, nothing can touch you.

CHAPTER EIGHT

JESUS SENDS PETER FISHING FOR MONEY

God takes care of His children.

Matthew 17:24-27

One time, Peter was out on a walk. And some men asked him a question that stumped him.

These men collected the money that was used to take care of God's temple. It was called the temple tax. "Peter," the men asked, "does your friend Jesus pay the temple tax like everyone else?"

Hmm, Peter thought. *Jesus always does the right thing. I'm sure Jesus pays the temple tax too.*

Peter answered. "Yes, I think He does." And the men walked off.

When he got back home, before

he could say one single itty-bitty word, Jesus said: "What do you think about the temple tax, Peter?"

How did Jesus know what Peter was thinking? But of course Jesus knew. He knows every single thing we ever think!

But Jesus wasn't done asking questions. (He always asks good questions.)

"Peter," Jesus asked, "when kings collect taxes, do their sons and daughters pay them? Or do other people pay them?"

"No, Jesus," Peter answered. "They're royalty— princes and princesses! Kids don't pay their dad. Other people pay the king."

"That's right!" Jesus answered. "You see, the temple is my Dad's house. And we're His kids, princes and princesses. So we don't really have to pay the temple tax. But we don't want to upset those tax collectors. So here's what I want you to do. Go fishing. And the first fish you catch, look in its mouth. There will be a coin there. It'll be just enough money to pay the tax for Me and you."

Jesus smiled. But Peter was confused. Really confused.

Jesus wants me to go fishing because a fish is going to give me money? Peter wondered. *He can't be serious.*

But when Peter looked at Jesus, he could tell that Jesus meant what He said. So Peter grabbed his fishing pole and off he went.

Now, how am I going to catch a fish with a coin in its mouth? Peter thought as he walked along. *Am I going to catch him on his way home from the fish bank or something?*

When Peter got to the beach, he breathed in the sea air. *Ahh, home.* A little fishy, but he didn't mind one bit. He baited his hook, and cast his line out into the water.

Tug, tug, tug. A fish! Carefully, carefully, he pulled it in. And sure enough, there was something stuck in its mouth–a silver coin! Just the right amount of money to pay the temple tax for two people.

Peter threw the fish back into the sea. He stood on the seashore, looking at the coin. He was shocked. Flabbergasted. Gobsmacked. Then up bubbled a chuckle. Then another. Then a full-blown laugh. Soon Peter just couldn't control himself. He laughed and snorted so hard his sides hurt.

Jesus had made sure that there would be a coin in this fish's mouth! Then He made sure that exact fish hopped on Peter's line. It was all so silly, and it was all Jesus' idea.

You see, Jesus could have made the temple tax money they needed back at Peter's house. After all, He created everything! But Jesus wanted Peter to obey even when God's commands seemed silly. And He wanted Peter to remember that God would always take care of his needs– sometimes in amazing ways! Plus, Peter had a fish story he would never forget!

CHAPTER NINE

THE DAD WHO NEVER STOPS LOVING

God always runs to welcome you home.

Luke 15:11-32

Once Jesus told a story about a dad with two sons. The dad loved his sons—he had buckets and buckets of love for them. But the younger son didn't care. He was tired of chopping the wood, milking the cows, feeding the sheep.

"Dad," he told his father one day, arms crossed. "I don't want to be here anymore. Give me your money. I'm leaving."

The dad's heart broke right in two. You see, this was the money that his son would be given after he died. "I wish you were gone, Dad," the son was saying. "I don't love you." There's nothing worse than that.

The son took the money and went to a far country. Life was good! He threw the best parties with the most scrumptious food and the tastiest drinks. Party, party, party every night!

But back home, the dad's heart was still broken. At the end of every day, he would stand outside, staring down the road, looking for his runaway son, longing for his return. *Please, please come home to me, my boy,* the dad thought.

Back in the faraway country, things got bad. The son ran out of money. The country ran out of food. So there were no more parties. No more meals. No more fun. The son had to find a job, but the only one he could find was feeding muddy, stinky pigs.

This pig slop sure looks good, the son thought as he sloshed out the pigs' muck one morning. He was so hungry. *Maybe the owner won't notice if I have just a teeny, tiny bite.*

He leaned down and put his face near the trough. *Scarf, scarf, scarf,* the pigs snorted as they ate. The son got a whiff of the gloppy slop. *What am I thinking? Here I am about to eat pig slop while the people who work for my dad have lots of food. And I'm his son! I can't believe I left—my dad was so good to me. I've got to go home and tell him how sorry I am.*

All the way home, the son practiced and practiced his speech. "Dad, I'm so sorry. I probably can't be your son anymore. But I miss you. Please just let me work for you."

He let out a deep breath before he crossed over the last hill home. *Sigh.* But the minute his head popped over the hill, his dad saw him. Because, of course, he was looking for him.

"My son! My son!" the dad cried, running as fast as he could. The father threw his arms around his son in the biggest, tightest bear hug.

The son started

his please-take-me-back speech. "Dad, I'm so sorry. I probably can't be your son anymore–"

His father shushed him. "Quick!" he called to his workers, "My son is home! Bring the best clothes, bring the family ring! My son is home! We'll have the biggest party ever! I thought my son was dead, but he's come home alive!"

But the dad had two sons, remember? When the other son came home from working and saw the robe, the ring, and the party, he got very upset. "Dad," he told his father. "I've been here all along, working hard. I've done everything you asked. But you've never done anything this wonderful for me. And I've been good!"

The father's heart broke again. "Oh, my son," he said. "Can't you see how much I love you? Everything I have is yours, and it always has been. I love your brother, yes, but I love you just as much."

You see, the father wanted to show his sons what love really means. The younger son left home, but came back and found his dad still loved him. The dad loved the older son, too, but not because he obeyed all the rules. He loved both his sons because he was their dad!

Jesus told this story because God is your Father, who loves you like that dad loved his sons. If you run away, He wants you to come home. If you do everything right, He still wants you to come home. He loves you more than you can ever imagine. In fact, God loves you so much that He sent His Son to rescue you and bring you home to be with Him forever. That's what true love is!

CHAPTER TEN

THE HURT AND HOORAY DAY

Jesus is even stronger than death.

John 11

Cough, cough. Cough, cough. Lazarus was sick. Really sick. And he wasn't getting any better.

"We should let Jesus know," his sister Mary said. "Jesus heals sick people all the time."

So Mary and her sister Martha sent a message to Jesus. Then they waited for Him to come.

And they waited.

And they waited.

You see, Jesus was far away when the message got to Him.

"Our friend Lazarus is going to be just fine," Jesus told His disciples. "God is going to use this sickness to show how good He is." So Jesus' disciples didn't think a thing about it.

"It's time to go to see Lazarus," Jesus said two whole days later. "He has gone to sleep, but I'm going to wake him up."

"Jesus," His friends answered. "If Lazarus is sleeping, that's great! He'll wake up and feel better."

The disciples thought that Lazarus was taking a nap.

So Jesus told them the news: "Lazarus has died. It's time to go see him."

They headed to Bethany, where Lazarus had lived. "Jesus!" Martha said, running out to Him. "You're too late. Lazarus died days ago! But if You had been here, I know You could have made him better!"

"Don't worry, Martha." Jesus said. "Your brother is going to live again."

"I know he is," Martha answered. "God will raise us all back to life when the broken days are over."

"You don't have to wait until then," Jesus answered. "I'm fixing what's broken now! I am the Life-Giver. Believe in Me, and you don't have to be afraid of death."

"I believe." Martha answered. "I really do!"

Soon, Mary came to Jesus, too. A crowd of crying people followed her, another sad parade.

Jesus looked around at all the people. Their eyes were filled with tears. Their hearts were filled with pain. And Jesus got angry. Death is awful, terrible! And it shouldn't be! You see, in God's Kingdom, no one ever dies. And no one is ever, ever sad.

"Please take me to Lazarus' tomb," Jesus said. *Sniff, sniff, sob, sob,* Jesus joined the sad parade. As He saw how everyone's hearts were aching, and His heart ached too. Tears slid down His cheeks.

Once at the tomb, Jesus got angry at death again. "Move that rock away from the tomb!" He said.

"Jesus," Martha whispered. "Lazarus has been dead for four days. It's going to be smelly."

"Don't you remember, Martha?" he said. "Remember how I said that if you believe in Me, then you will see how good God is?"

When the rock was moved, Jesus prayed. "Father God, death has happened here to one of Your children, and I know that You hate that. I'm praying out loud so the people here will know that You are the One who is about to show how great You are."

Jesus paused. Then He shouted: "Lazarus, come out!"

Everyone waited, and then someone appeared at the door of the tomb! Out walked a man–wrapped up in cloth like a mummy! Lazarus!

"Get those graveclothes off," Jesus said, smiling as everybody cheered. "He won't be needing those anymore."

Hooray! Jesus is stronger than death! In fact, Jesus is stronger than any hard thing. But He knows what it's like to be sad for your friends, to hurt when they hurt. Even though Jesus knew Lazarus would live again, He hurt because His friends were hurting.

Jesus knows your story, too. Your life will end in one big hooray, too. And even when hard things happen in your life, He is up to something good. He knows everything is going to turn out just fine, and you can trust Him. But He also sees when you hurt, inside and out. And because He loves you so much, He hurts with you.

So you can go to Jesus with all of your hoorays, and He will laugh with you. But you can also go to Him with all of your hurts. And He will cry with you. And one day–one great day–He will make all your hurts into hoorays. And you will never cry or say "ouch" again!

CHAPTER ELEVEN

THE BLIND MAN WHO REALLY SAW

God wants you to come to Him with what you need.
Mark 10:46-52

One day, Jesus and His 12 friends were leaving a city called Jericho. A large crowd was following Jesus, as crowds often did.

A man was sitting outside the city gates. His name was Bartimaeus, but people might have called him Blind Bart. You see, Bart's eyes were broken. He couldn't see colors. He couldn't see trees. He couldn't see his best friends or his mom or his dad or anything else. He saw nothing but black darkness all the time.

But Bart wanted to see, more than anything! Every day, Bart sat near the gates outside the city. Sadly, since Bart couldn't see, he couldn't work. Since he couldn't work, he didn't have money for food or clothes or anything else. So he sat near the city gates, where people came and went each day, and asked the people who passed by to help him out.

Now even though Bart's eyes didn't work, his ears worked just fine. Most days he could hear the crowds of people as they walked in and out of the city. But today he heard something new.

"It's Jesus!" he heard someone say.

Jesus! Jesus could fix my eyes so I can see! Bart thought. *This is my chance! But I've got to get His attention.* So Bart started yelling and yelling.

"Jesus, son of David! *Jesus!* JESUS!" he hollered. "You're the Rescuer we have been waiting for! Have mercy on me!" Which was Bart's way of saying "Please see me and help me!"

"Shh!" someone said. "Be quiet! Stop hollering!"

"You're making such a ruckus," said another. "We want to hear Jesus, not you!"

But Bart ignored them, and kept right on crying out.

"Jesus, son of David! *Jesus!* JESUS!" he yelled, even louder this time. "Help me! Have mercy on me!"

Bart took a deep breath to yell again, but as he did, he heard the crowd stop moving. No one talked, no feet shuffled.

"Tell him to come here," a voice said, and Bart worried that he was in real trouble now.

"Cheer up!" the people said. "Jesus wants to see you!"

Bart's heart jumped sky high! Jesus wanted to see him! He threw aside his coat and leapt up as fast as he could. He felt his way through the crowd, the people helping him along, until he stood before Jesus.

"What would you like Me to do for you?" asked the kindest voice Bart had ever heard.

"Jesus!" Blind Bart cried. "My eyes are broken. But I really want to see. Please help me!"

"Even though your eyes can't see, you saw the truth about Me," Jesus said. "You knew I would be able to heal you. You believed in Me, and that has fixed your eyes!"

Bart blinked, and when he opened his eyes, he could see! And the first thing he saw was the most beautiful thing he would ever see: the smiling face of Jesus.

Blindness—or anything that's broken—isn't the way that God wants it. God is perfectly good, so in His kingdom, everyone's eyes work perfectly—no one even needs glasses! And God's kingdom came to Bart that day.

Even more amazing is that Jesus asked Bart, "What do you want Me to do for you?" Jesus knew what Bart needed—Jesus knows everything! But He invited Bart to talk about his needs and ask Jesus for help.

It's just the same with us. Jesus knows every single thing that you need, and He wants to help you! But He loves for you to come to Him and share what's on your heart. After all, good friends share their hearts with each other, and Jesus wants to be your very best friend. He wants you to tell Him what you need. And when the answer comes, you'll know deep, deep down in your heart that *Jesus* answered—Jesus, your good Friend, who loves you very much.

CHAPTER TWELVE

HOW JESUS HANDLES STINKY THINGS

Jesus loves you, so He did the hardest thing for you.
John 13; Luke 22:39-54

Jesus and His twelve disciples were eating a special meal together. As they ate, they retold the story of how God had rescued their many-times-great-grandparents from the land of Egypt. "God rescued us, remember?" they said.

While they were eating, Jesus did something odd. He got up from the table, wrapped a towel around His waist, and filled a bowl with water. Then He went around the table and washed His friends' dirty feet.

Splish. Squish. Scrub.

Now, you see, people's feet were *really* dirty back then.

Everyone walked around in sandals all day on dirt roads—the same roads that sheep and horses and camels traveled. Dust and dirt and other disgusting stuff got stuck on their feet and in between their toes. So everyone's feet were filthy, yucky, hold-your-nose stinky.

In those days, when you went over to someone's house, it was good manners for your host to have someone wash the road yuck off your feet. But because the job was smelly, only the lowest of the low people did it: the servants. So it was very odd when Jesus—the King, the most important Person—got on His knees and began to scrub his friends' feet.

When Jesus took Peter's feet in His hands and started to wash them, Peter couldn't stand it. "Jesus, don't!" he cried.

"Peter," Jesus said, "I've got to wash you so you can be close to Me."

You see, just as God had rescued His people from the mean Egyptians, Jesus had come to rescue them again. Sin had made their hearts dirtier than their feet, and they couldn't come close to God with dirty hearts.

Peter and the disciples thought Jesus was just washing feet. But He was really helping them to see something beautiful and true about His work. "I'm going to wash your hearts clean just as I'm washing your filthy feet," He was saying.

Jesus washed the feet of all 12 of His friends. But one man at the table wasn't really a friend at all: Judas. He had a plan to do something awful. There were people who didn't like Jesus and wanted to hurt Him. Judas was going to help these people capture Jesus.

Finally, Jesus turned to Judas and said, "Go and do what you planned." So Judas went out into the night. No one else understood what was happening.

Once the meal was over, Jesus and His friends left to go to their favorite place, a garden full of olive trees. As they walked, Jesus told them what was about to happen next. "I'm going to leave you for a time," he said. "The hardest part of my work comes next, but then your hearts will be washed clean!"

Once they got to the garden of olive trees, Jesus grew very sad. You see, in order to rescue everyone, He was going to carry everyone's sins. Every bad deed, every mean thought, every evil lie. It was a dirty job, one that a King shouldn't have to do, but He would crush that serpent's head, just as God promised way back in the beginning!

Jesus knew what He had to do, but it was still hard. So He went to be alone with His Father. "Father!" He prayed, crying big tears. "Father, I'm scared about what I need to do. But I love You, and I will do whatever You ask.

Clank, clank. Stomp, stomp. An angry mob of soldiers was trudging into the garden. Judas had led them straight to Jesus. And Jesus let them arrest Him. He let the mean people take Him to do the awful thing they were planning. Even though He was so very sad, He trusted God. And even though His heart was breaking, it was also filled with love for all of us. He was ready to clean our sin-stained hearts.

CHAPTER THIRTEEN

THE MOST AWFUL BEST DAY

Jesus paid for your sins so you can be His friend forever.
Matthew 27: 11-66

The soldiers marched Jesus from the garden of olive trees and took Him to the people who hated Him. These people were jealous of Jesus. The crowds were listening to Jesus instead of them! They put Jesus on trial like He was a criminal, even though Jesus had never, ever done anything wrong. The judges said He was guilty, that He was a criminal. They said He would have to die.

After the trial, soldiers led Him away. The soldiers began to make fun of Jesus. "You say You're a king, eh?" they said. "Well, a king needs a royal robe." And they put a purple robe on Jesus. "Kings carry royal scepters," they said next, and put a stick in Jesus' hand. "And kings wear crowns." They made a crown of sharp thorns and pushed it down on Jesus' head. It hurt so much!

It must have hurt very much, but Jesus didn't fight back. These men had broken hearts, too, and Jesus would even wash their hearts clean.

The soldiers made Jesus carry a wooden cross through the

streets and up a steep hill. At the top, they used nails to hang Jesus on the cross.

Crowds surrounded the cross, and people shouted mean things at Him.

"You can't be the Son of God!" they yelled. "God wouldn't let this happen!"

They shouted hateful things at Him. It was awful. It was terrible. But in the midst of it all, Jesus was obeying His Father. He was finishing His mission, the one planned from the very beginning. Jesus was making a way for people's hearts to be clean and new, forever. Your heart. Mine. Everyone's!

No one in the crowds could see the angels watching. They knew what

was happening.

The sky grew dark, dark, dark. It too knew what was happening. Jesus was facing down all the evil in the world.

"If You are God's Son, save Yourself!" some people around Him cried. "Get down from that cross!"

And the people were right. Jesus really could have saved Himself. He could have hopped off that cross and healed all of His wounds in an

instant. He could have called all those angels to come fight for Him—they were ready. He could have, but He didn't.

You see, Jesus chose to let the people hurt Him. (Remember what God told the serpent?) He didn't fight back. Jesus was taking the blame for our sins, even though He had done nothing wrong. And He let those judges, those soldiers, those people treat him like a criminal, even though He was perfectly good. Why? Because He wanted to! Because He knew it was the only way we could ever have clean hearts. Feeling all of this pain and shame and awfulness was worth it to Jesus, if it could save us. He loves us that much.

The sky grew dark, as dark as night, even though it was afternoon. And Jesus felt all alone, sadder even than He had felt in the garden of olive trees.

But just when it seemed darkest, Jesus cried, "It is finished!" And then He let go of His life. He died.

Suddenly, the ground shook. Lightning split the sky. It was as if the earth just couldn't bear what had happened. Everything really *did* seem finished! And then it was over.

A little later, two of Jesus' friends came to get Him down from the cross. They placed His body in a garden tomb, a cave cut out of the rock. They rolled a huge stone in front of its entrance.

And just to make sure, Jesus' enemies placed guards at the tomb. They thought Jesus' friends might plan something sneaky, and they didn't want anyone to get in. They didn't stop to think that Someone might get out.

CHAPTER FOURTEEN

THE DAY JESUS WON IT ALL

Jesus rose from the dead so you can have new life.
Matthew 28:1-8; Luke 24:36-49; John 20:1-23

*J*esus' friends were sad, sad, sad. Jesus was gone. Could anything worse have happened? They gathered together and gave each other hugs and cried. Theirs was the saddest house in the city.

For three days, Jesus' tomb was quiet. The guards outside didn't have much to do. But then, early Sunday morning, out of the blue, the earth started shaking. And shaking. And shaking! An angel, bright as the sun, appeared at the tomb. He rolled the huge, heavy stone away as easily as if it was a tiny pebble. Then he sat down on top of it, waiting.

This was all too much for the guards. They fell over like toppled trees. *Timber!*

At the sad house, Mary Magdalene stood up, drying her eyes. "We should go to Jesus' tomb," she said to her friends. Mary loved Jesus so much. He had healed her, and she had followed Him every day since. So, of course, Mary wanted to go and visit Jesus' tomb. Because that's what you do when you miss your dear friend.

Once Mary and the other women got to the tomb, their mouths fell open. The stone was moved, and the cave's black mouth gaped. They peered inside—no Jesus! Where was He?

Suddenly, a light bright as a thousand suns shone all around them, as bright as that long-ago night when the shepherds heard about Jesus' birth. The angel! "Why are you looking for Jesus in the tomb?" he asked the surprised women. "Tombs are for dead people. And Jesus isn't dead! He has come back to life! He promised He would, and He has!"

Jesus is alive? Mary couldn't believe it. It was too wonderful!

"Go and tell the others," the angel said. So Mary and the women took off as fast as they could back to the saddest house.

"He's alive! He's alive!" they sang as they ran. They were so excited that they almost ran into a man on the road.

"Hello!" the man said, smiling. Was that voice familiar? When the man said her name, then she knew. This was the man who had fixed her horrible, broken life! And here He was … He had fixed the most horrible, broken thing there is—death!

It was Jesus! Hooray! It was Jesus! He was alive and well and perfectly fine! Hooray! Hooray! Hooray! There just weren't enough hoorays!

The women fell down at Jesus' feet. "Oh, Jesus! You're here!" they said as they cried, but they weren't crying sad tears at all. Just like Jesus does, He turned their sad tears into happy ones.

Jesus laughed, and the joy of it echoed all the way down to their toes. "Go tell our friends I'm alive," He said. "I will meet up with you in a little while."

The women ran as fast as they could to the sad house. *Pound, pound, pound,* they knocked on the door. Peter answered it, and the women burst in. Everyone around had tear-streaked faces and sad, sad hearts. "Jesus is alive!" the women shouted, talking on top of each other. "We've seen Him! We've talked to Him!"

Jesus was alive! And you could almost see it as the news sank in to everyone's hearts: the dark sadness was melting away. The crying could end! All of a sudden, the saddest house became the happiest house!

Later, Jesus joined the party Himself. "I'll take some fish!" he said, and the party got even more joyful. Jesus was not only alive, but he had a real body! This one would never get hurt or sick or die. God promised to make everything–and everyone–happy and new!

Jesus is still alive today! Jesus gave his life to rescue you and me and everyone who would believe in Him. But He didn't stay dead–He rose to life! He fought death, and He won! And the prize was the best thing ever: everything! Because Jesus won it all, you can be free from sin and free to live close to God.

CHAPTER FIFTEEN

GOD'S MOVE-IN DAY

Jesus sent His Holy Spirit so He would always be with you.

Acts 1:1-11, Acts 2:1-41

For 40 days, Jesus stayed with His friends, teaching them more about God. One day while they were eating a picnic lunch, Jesus told them: "It's almost time for me to leave. But my Father and I will send Someone very special to you. The Holy Spirit is going to come and live in your hearts! He will keep teaching you after I've gone."

Chew, chew, chew. Smack, smack, smack. All of His friends nodded along, munching on their lunches. But then, something amazing happened.

Jesus started going up, up, up into the sky! The disciples watched Him go until a cloud got in the way. The disciples just stood there with their mouths open, staring up for a long, long time.

"Why are you just sitting there, looking up to the sky?" the disciples heard someone say. They saw two angels standing nearby. "Jesus has gone," he explained, "but don't worry! He'll be back!"

The disciples were confused, but they were happy, too. Jesus had finished his rescue mission! Every day for the next few days, Jesus' friends gathered and prayed, praising God for what He had done, and asking Him to guide them. They knew the Holy Spirit would be coming soon.

One day while they were together, when *whoosh!* It sounded as if a strong wind was blowing. Then something strange happened—flames in the shape of tongues appeared above them! They separated into little flames and landed on each person—but they didn't hurt.

Suddenly, each one of Jesus' friends felt very happy, like new life was bubbling up inside them. God's Holy Spirit was making a home in their hearts, just as Jesus had promised! He would heal their broken hearts. He would help them remember what Jesus taught. And He would remind them that they belonged to God, who loved them very much.

After God's Spirit moved into His friends' hearts that day, something strange happened. They started speaking in other languages–languages they didn't know! Imagine trying to say hello to your friend, but it came out "Bonjour!" (That's "hello" in French.)

People who were in town for the feast wondered, *Why are strangers speaking our languages?* They flocked to see what was going on.

Peter knew, and God made him brave and gave him just the right words to say. "Everyone," he said. "I know you're wondering how we can speak your languages. I'll tell you why: It's God's Holy Spirit! God loves you, and He wants you to hear, in your own language, how you can be His friend!"

"We want to be God's friends," many people in the crowd said. "What should we do?"

"You have to ask God to forgive you for your sins," Peter answered. "And He will give you a new heart. God's Son Jesus came and died so that you could hear God say, 'I forgive you.' But He rose from the dead so you could live a new life with Him! And now His Spirit can live in your clean heart–just as He's living in ours! And you can be God's friend forever!"

So many people wanted to become God's friends that day–3,000 of them! They were all baptized and became part of God's family!

If you're God's friend, God's Spirit lives in you, too! If you ask, He will help you to hear God's voice, and to tell other people about God's love. That's what He loves to do when He moves in.

CHAPTER SIXTEEN

THE DAY THE WORLD LOOKED MORE LIKE HOME

God wants you to help make the world look more like His kingdom.

Acts 3-4

Jesus had gone back home to heaven, but He hadn't really left His friends. His Spirit was living right inside their hearts! He was as close as close can be. And the world was about to see what God can do with His friends.

One day, Peter and John were walking to the temple to pray. Outside of one of the temple gates, they saw a man whose legs had never, ever worked for his entire life—40 whole years! Every day, his friends would carry him to one of the gates, hoping that the people passing by would give him money for food and clothes.

"Please help me," the man begged. "My legs don't work." Every once in a while, people would toss money into his plate. *Clink, clink.*

When Peter and John came close, the man begged, "Please, I need money." He kept his head low to the ground.

"Look up at us!" Peter said. And when the man looked up, his sad eyes saw Peter's kind face smiling right back at him.

"I don't have any money," Peter explained, "but I have something much better to give you. Jesus wants your legs to work. So in the name of Jesus—work, legs! Work!"

Before the man could think much about what Peter had said, Peter pulled him to his feet. He could stand! He took one step, then two. "Woo-hoo!" he shouted. "My legs! My legs work!" He jumped around like a rabbit, hooting and hollering and thanking God. "Thank You, God! Thank You, thank You, thank You!" He just couldn't say enough thank-yous!

Everyone saw the ruckus, and crowded around Peter, and God's Spirit made him brave again.

"My friends," Peter called out, "don't be surprised at me. I didn't fix this man's legs. God did it, through the power of Jesus' name. God loves you, too, and He wants to fix what's broken in your life—starting

with your heart."

Some leaders heard what Peter and John were teaching. They didn't like it one bit. These were the same leaders who were jealous of Jesus and had Him killed. So they ordered Peter and John arrested and put into prison.

The next morning, the leaders brought John and Peter before them. "How did you heal that man's legs?" they asked.

"Leaders," Peter responded, feeling the Holy Spirit giving him courage. "Listen to me. Jesus' power healed this man's legs! God wants to fix everything that's broken." The leaders weren't happy with what Peter was saying. But he kept on speaking, because God's Spirit made him bold.

"Even though you helped kill Jesus, God loves you. There's no other way you can be God's friend than to receive the clean heart and new life Jesus wants to give you."

Grumble, grumble, grumble. The leaders' hearts were too hard for God's love to get in. But they could see the man with fixed legs, and they couldn't argue with that. "What are we going to do about these men?" they said to each other. "We've got to stop them or everyone is going to follow Jesus and not us!"

The leaders spoke to Peter and John once again. "No more teaching about Jesus!"

But Peter and John wouldn't listen. "We can't stop telling people about Jesus. He wants everyone to know how much He loves them! You can arrest us over and over, but we obey God, not you."

After one more warning, the leaders let Peter and John go. They went home to the other Jesus-followers, who were so happy when they heard how God had fixed the man's legs. It was so fun to have God do such great things!

God wants the world to look more like His kingdom—more like heaven. His kingdom is where everything is whole and happy and good—where legs work!—and where people know how much God loves them. Peter and John wanted everyone to see God's good heart, so they shared it, no matter what!

That's just what God wants you to do, too! When His Holy Spirit inside of you speaks up and says, "Hey, that doesn't look the way God wants it to," then it's time to do something! Ask God to help you figure out what to do, and then do it. You can make the world look more like God's kingdom and help people see His love!

CHAPTER SEVENTEEN

WHEN JESUS CHANGED A MAN'S LIFE—AND HIS NAME

God wants you to share Jesus and His great love with everyone.

Acts 9

Saul frowned at every follower of Jesus he saw. *They've got it all wrong about God,* he thought. *I've got to get them.*

But Saul was the one who had gotten it all wrong. Saul had followed God his whole life. He had even been to a special school to learn God's Word. But somehow in all of his studying and do-gooding, Saul had misunderstood God's heart. He was wrong about Jesus.

So Jesus decided to introduce Himself! One day, Saul and his friends were heading to a town called Damascus to arrest followers of Jesus. They were walking along a dusty road when, *flash!* The sky lit up around them. It was so bright, so powerful, so awesome, that Saul's legs wouldn't hold him up anymore. Down he fell–*thud!*

"Saul, Saul!" a voice boomed. "Why are you doing this to Me?"

"Who are You?" Saul asked from the ground.

"I am Jesus," the voice answered. "You think you're helping God, but you're hurting My friends, and *Me.* And that means you're working *against* God. Now go into Damascus, and I'll let you know what to do next."

Saul's friends just stood there, their mouths wide open. They had heard the voice, too! They helped Saul get up from the ground, but when he opened his eyes–

"I can't see!" he exclaimed. Then his friends took him by the hand and he stumbled along, blind, into Damascus.

Since Saul couldn't see, he had plenty of time to think and to talk with God. For three whole days, he didn't eat, and he didn't drink. He just talked to God about all of the things he had gotten wrong.

Meanwhile, a man named Ananias was in that same town talking to God, too. "Ananias!" God said to him, and Ananias answered, "I'm right here, Lord!"

"A man named Saul is staying at a house on Straight Street," the Lord said. "He's praying. I've told him that I'm sending you to him. Now, go, put your hands on him, and pray for him, and I will give him his sight back."

"God, I'm afraid!" Ananias said, "I've heard about this Saul. He arrests people who follow You!"

"Don't be afraid to go," God answered. "I've chosen Saul to go all over and tell people about Me."

"Okay, Lord. I'll do it." So away Ananias went, straight to the house on Straight Street. *Knock, knock, knock.* Inside, kneeling on the floor, Ananias found Saul praying, just like God had said!

"Saul," Ananias said, "on the road into town, Jesus introduced Himself to you. He loves you so much! He sent me to see you filled with the Holy Spirit–and to bring back your sight!"

Right away, something like hard scales fell off his eyes, and Saul could see. And as the Holy Spirit came into his heart, he could really see.

"I've been so wrong!" Saul said. "Jesus is the Rescuer and the Lord of everything. Please baptize me!" And Ananias did.

Saul started telling anyone who would listen that Jesus was Lord. At first, people weren't sure Saul had changed. But they soon realized that the Holy Spirit had changed Saul forever. He was so different that people started using Saul's other name: Paul.

Paul never stopped telling anyone and everyone how God had changed him, and how God wants to do the same for everyone. He started many churches so people could learn about Jesus. He also wrote letters to his friends, teaching them how to know and follow Jesus better. We can still read some of those letters in the Bible!

Paul knew God's love from experience, because Jesus had met him on the road to Damascus. He faced some hard times, but no matter what happened, he kept telling people about God and His great love. God wants you to tell others, too! Many people in your world don't know Jesus. You can introduce them to Him! Just love them like God does, and when they ask why you're so kind, tell them that God loves them so much and wants to be their friend forever.

CHAPTER EIGHTEEN

THE LAST OUCH

Jesus is going to fix every broken thing, and you will live with Him forever.
Revelation 19–21

The world and the angels watched as Jesus let Himself be nailed to the cross for every sin. The sky cracked, and the world shook and broke under the weight of it all. "It is finished!" He cried when it was all over, and He died.

But three days later, Jesus' heart started beating again. *Pump-pump. Pump-pump. Pump-pump.* He came back to life! All of that sin? He had paid for it all. And death? He had defeated it. Now, he offered the greatest gift ever to all who would listen. "I have clean hearts and new life for anyone who wants them!" He said. "You can be God's friend forever!"

But wait. Things are still not quite right, are they? People still hurt, and get hurt, and we say words like *ouch*. People get sick, and things die, and we're so sad that we cry. God didn't make the world to be this way. They're bent, or broken, because we live in a world that's still being fixed.

And God promised that His story isn't over. From the very beginning, God told Adam and Eve that the serpent would be crushed. God promised that one day, everything would be made right. On that day, the sky will crack open again, but not in sadness. The world will shake again, but

not in pain. A white horse will appear, carrying a strong, powerful rider: Jesus! Like the greatest Hero, He is good and fair and true. He will lead God's armies, clothed in white like Him and riding on white horses. And Jesus' name will be on His robe: "King of Kings and Lord of Lords."

Jesus is such a good King that He's angry at all that's bad—anything that has ever hurt anybody, anything that has ever made them sad. His words will be like a sword, quick as a flash, and go to war against evil.

As soon as the battle begins, our Hero Jesus will win. Satan, that sneaky serpent, that wicked dragon, won't stand a chance against Jesus. He will be captured and thrown into a lake. Only this lake won't be made of water. It will be made of fire. He will stay there forever. So God's enemy— our enemy—who has whispered so many things to our hearts to make us

75

feel sad or unbeautiful or unloved, will never speak to us again. Hooray!

In those days, God will sit on a huge, white throne. Everyone who has ever lived will stand before Him. God will open the Book of Life, a special book He has been writing in for a long, long time. There He's written the names of every one of His friends. And you and me and all of God's friends will be so happy that our names are in His book and that we can be His friend forever.

Then God is going to do one more thing that He has been waiting a long, long time to do. He is going to bring heaven–His Kingdom, His home–down to earth. It's a beautiful, perfect garden city. God and His friends–that's us!–will be together again forever.

"Look," God will say, "I am fixing everything that's been broken, in heaven and earth! I'm making it all brand-new!" We will never hide from God again, the way Adam and Eve did. We will never cry sad tears again, the way God's people did in Egypt. We will never be afraid again, the way Jesus' friends were after He

died. We'll feel God's love all of the time! He'll give us brand new bodies that can't get sick or hurt or die. The last ouch will be over, forever. Hooray!

For the rest of time, you and me and all of God's friends will be together with God in a place that's as good as good can be. We'll play and laugh and live and love. We will never be able to say enough hoorays! We'll be home at last, the way God planned for us to be. Forever.

Come soon, Lord Jesus! We can't wait to be with You!

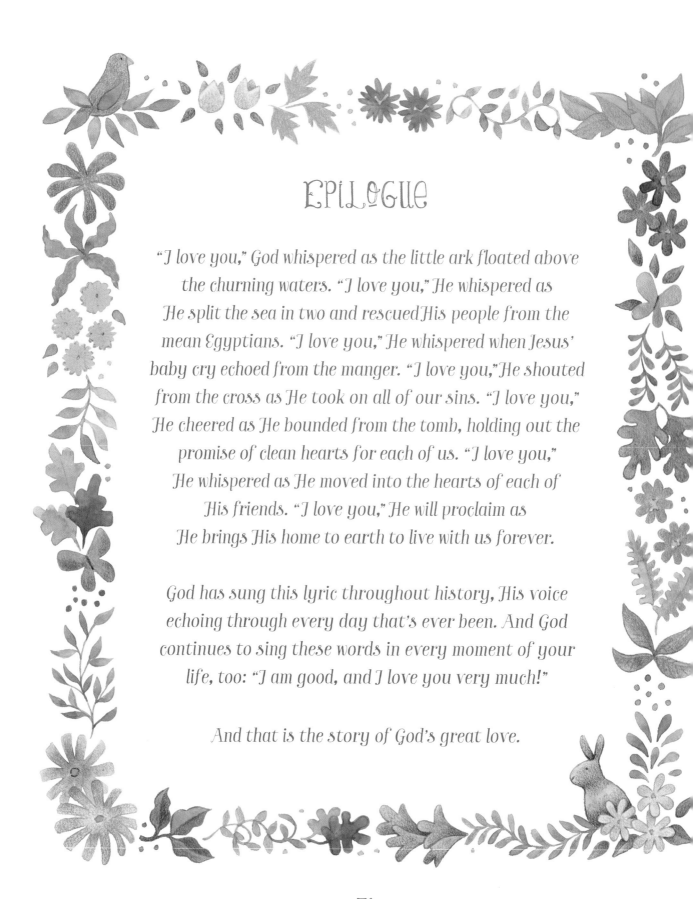

EPILOGUE

"I love you," God whispered as the little ark floated above the churning waters. "I love you," He whispered as He split the sea in two and rescued His people from the mean Egyptians. "I love you," He whispered when Jesus' baby cry echoed from the manger. "I love you," He shouted from the cross as He took on all of our sins. "I love you," He cheered as He bounded from the tomb, holding out the promise of clean hearts for each of us. "I love you," He whispered as He moved into the hearts of each of His friends. "I love you," He will proclaim as He brings His home to earth to live with us forever.

God has sung this lyric throughout history, His voice echoing through every day that's ever been. And God continues to sing these words in every moment of your life, too: "I am good, and I love you very much!"

And that is the story of God's great love.

A WORD FROM THE AUTHOR

LAURIN GRECO: As a mother, I feel there are two foundational truths that I strive to plant deep within my child's heart: *God is good,* and *He loves you very much.* So in each of these New Testament stories, I put a spotlight on God's heart to help kids see the goodness that's already there.

I wrote this Bible storybook for parents like me, and for grandparents—so we can take hold of every opportunity we have to train up a generation rooted in God's goodness and in His great love.

A WORD FROM THE ILLUSTRATOR

JEFF GREGORY: It was important to me that the illustrations accurately reflect the biblical stories—as much as possible for a children's book. These stories may be a child's first exposure to God's Word, and the images they see can shape their understanding of Scripture for years to come. As a child's guide into the world of the Bible, my hope is to show them God's power and goodness through these drawings.

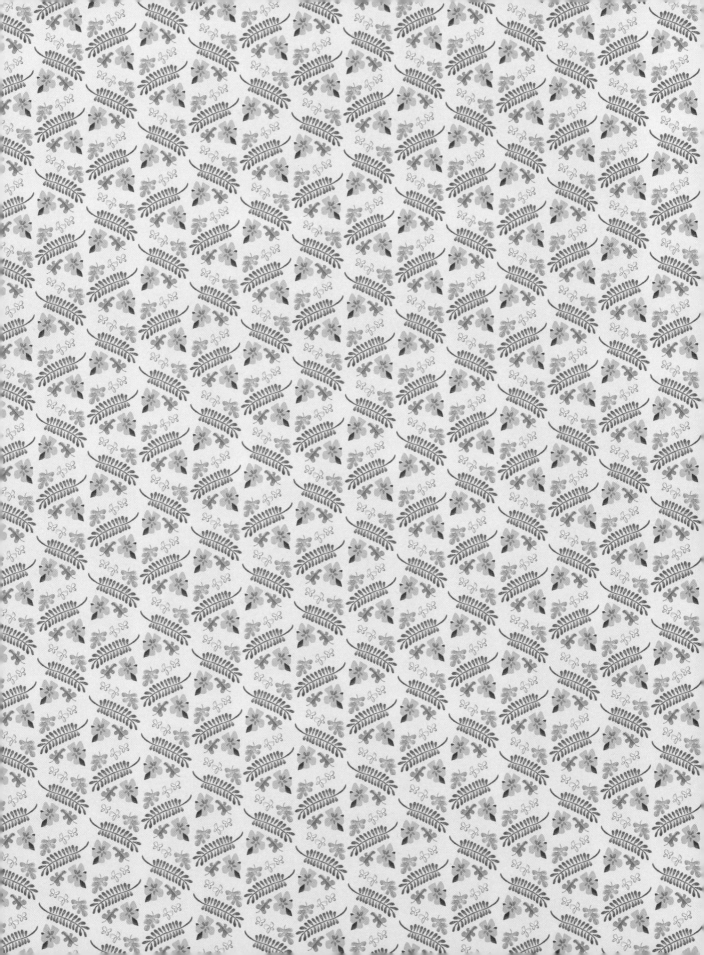

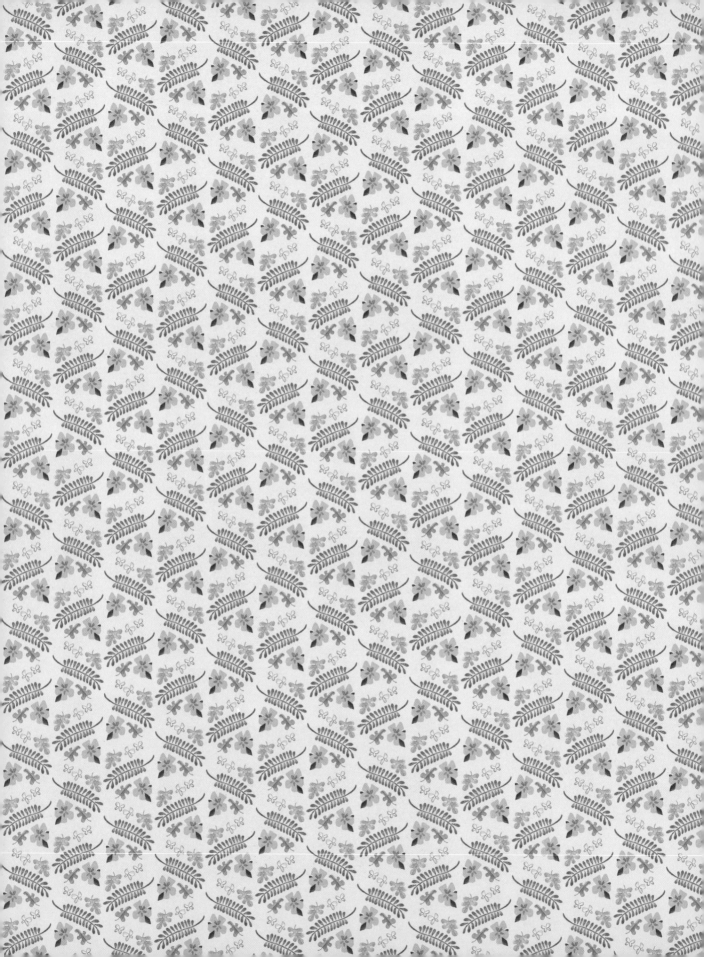